The POWER of Innocence

Warren Hunter

Sword Ministries International
Branson, Missouri

Unless otherwise indicated, all scriptural quotations are from *The New King James Version* of the Bible, Copyright © 1982 by Thomas Nelson, Inc.

Scripture verses marked AMP are taken from *The Amplified Bible*, Old Testament, copyright 1965, 1987 by Zondervan Corporation. *The Amplified Bible*, New Testament, Copyright © 1958, 1987 by Lockman Foundation. Used by permission.

Scripture verses marked RSV are taken from the *Revised Standard Version*, Old Testament Section, Copyright © 1952, New Testament Section, Copyright © 1946 by Division of Christian Education of the National Council of the Churches of Christ in the U.S.A.

Scripture verses marked NIV are taken from the *New International Version*, Copyright © 1973, 1978, 1984 by International Bible Society.

Scripture quotations marked NLT are taken from the *Holy Bible, New Living Translation* copyright © 1996 by Tyndale Charitable Trust.

The Power of Innocence
Published by:
Sword Ministries International
FMB 649
3044 Shepherd of the Hills
Exprwy No. 100
Branson, MO 65616
ISBN 1-889816-08-6

Cover design & book production by:
DB & Associates Design Group, Inc.
dba Double Blessings Productions
P.O. Box 52756, Tulsa, OK 74152
www.doubleblessing.com

Printed in the United States of America.

Contents

Contents

Introduction

When I was growing up in South Africa, we did not have television until I was thirteen years old. Before this, we enjoyed simple activities like playing with friends and the experiences that go along with life on a farm.

When I was six years old I came to the altar and asked Jesus into my heart. The following Sunday when my grandfather asked who wanted to be saved, I came to the altar again. After coming forward several times, my grandfather reminded me that once Jesus came into my heart, He would never leave me nor forsake me (Hebrews 13:5). When I came to the altar on the very next Sunday, my grandfather asked me why I kept coming to get saved? I replied, "I just love asking Jesus into my heart." This is the simplicity of innocence.

I will always remember when I was twelve years old. I stood in front of Roodeport Assembly of God in South Africa and gave my testimony. Afterwards Pastor Sam Ennis and my grandfather, Bernard Hunter, baptized me in water. About that same time, a lady named Sister Liendenberg prayed for me to receive the power of the Holy Spirit. I subsequently had an experience with the Holy Spirit where I prayed in tongues at the altar for five hours. My life was never the same again. From there, I began memorizing scripture and leading Bible Studies in high school. Although I didn't know it at the time, God was working a spirit of innocence within me.

My stepmother, Elise, gave me two books to read. One was "The Release of the Spirit" by Watchman Nee and the other was "Walking in the Paths of Jesus" by Whitney Pratney. Both of these books massively changed my life and out of these teaching experiences, was birthed my first book entitled "Keys To A Yielded Will."

If I dedicated this book to anyone, it would have to be my grandfather. His simplicity of heart touched my young life. While he was building a new church, I would run around the construction site playing. Occasionally I stopped and helped lay a few bricks because it was fun in my childish thinking. My heart was very innocent during those times.

During my second mother's death and before leaving for America, a bit of hardness came to my heart towards God. As a result, I began allowing my heart to be exposed to some things I wouldn't otherwise have seen.

When I came to America, I was bombarded with secular movies, unwholesome music and many other things that can only be described as evil in content. Even though I began attending Christian-based University, occasionally some of us watched R Rated movies with murder and other mayhem in them. During this time, it seemed as though my heart lost its sensitivity to the convicting power of the Holy Spirit. Towards the latter part of my sophomore year, God began to show me how my heart that had once been so innocent towards Him was being destroyed.

Within the last few years, I was visiting South Africa and someone gave me a copy of an old message called "The Price of Glory" that my wife and I had ministered together in 1993. As I listened to the message, I began weeping when I realized the power of my innocence during that time.

I asked the Lord what had happened to me. He revealed to me how the wounds of other pastors were working to destroy the innocent relationship I had with my heavenly Father. On that day the Lord began speaking to me about the power of innocence.

In order to be totally honest, I must say that if there ever was a nation in the world that lacks an understanding of the power of innocence, it is America. My prayer is that through this book you will see what true innocence involves and how it can be restored. He that hath an ear let him hear what the Spirit says.

I pray that just as God began to deal with me on this subject, He will deal in loving correction with each person that reads this book. I also encourage you to read my books "Unlimited Realm Vols. 1 & 2 which deal with unlimited forgiveness and unlimited love.

Chapter 1

The Innocence of a Child

And the LORD God formed man of the dust of the ground, and breathed into his nostrils the breath of life; and man became a living soul.

Genesis 2:7

It is interesting that the word "soul" in Genesis 2:7 is translated from the Hebrew word "nephish." It is not improper to translate "nephish" as "soul," but it has a much deeper meaning. "Nephish" also means *to take breath as if to literally draw breath from the Spirit of God. It is to be totally dependent upon God for everything, i.e., even the very breath that one takes*. The "nephish" or "soul" has no idea of either mortality or morality — it is totally innocent. There is no idea of corruption, death or decay in this word and certainly no idea of sin.

It is important to note that after the fall of Adam, the soul of man was no longer referred to as "nephish," but as "lev." The word "lev", which is also translated "soul" or "heart," contains the ideas of mortality, morality, sin, decay and corruption.

But as many as received Him, to them He gave the right to become children of God, even to those who believe in His name:

John 1:12

God didn't say He gave those who receive Him the right to become adults. He meant to use the word "children" in this verse because it refers to the innocence of a child. He gave those who will believe the right to become as innocent as children.

For you did not receive the spirit of bondage again to fear, but you received the Spirit of adoption by whom we cry out, "Abba, Father."

The Spirit Himself bears witness with our spirit that we are children of God,

and if children, then heirs — heirs of God and joint heirs with Christ, if indeed we suffer with Him, that we may also be glorified together.

Romans 8:15-17

God is your daddy. Understanding what this means is the root of unlimited power. It means you can take what the Word promises easily and innocently because your Father God gave it to you. You have no doubts you are His child.

Paul talked about the Corinthians moving in the gifts of the Spirit and yet he called them babes. Isn't it amazing that babies can move in the gifts of the Spirit? This is a powerful thought. Simplicity of heart is the essence of a child's innocence. It is about unimpaired purity. When you become a child of God, you have the authority, the power, the privilege and the right to everything concerning your Father. Innocence makes it easy for you to claim that. *We have been given the right to become the children of God.*

For you are all sons of God through faith in Christ Jesus. [in the anointing and Jesus who applied the blood to the mercy seat. Through that

2

which gives you access into the throne and the right to be a son].

✖ For as many of you as were baptized into Christ have put on Christ.

There is neither Jew nor Greek, there is neither slave nor free, there is neither male nor female; for you are all one in Christ Jesus.

And if you are Christ's, then you are Abraham's seed, and heirs according to the promise.

Galatians 3:26-29

The Bible tells us that all of the promises of God are yea and amen (2 Corinthians 1:20). They belong to us. Have you ever seen a child get into his daddy's shoes and walk around? Why do children do that? They do it because they want to be just like their daddy.

Innocence Will Imitate

Therefore be imitators of God as dear children.

Ephesians 5:1

In *Vine's Expository Dictionary of New Testament Words*, "Abba" is the word framed by the lips of infants, and betokens unreasoning trust; [whereas the word] "father" expresses an intelligent comprehension of the relationship. We are invited into a relationship of unreasoning trust with God. We should have the desire to walk in our Abba Father's shoes and act just like our Daddy. Jesus was bruised for our iniquities. Once iniquity is dealt with, we will have no problem walking in innocence.

If I promise my little boy something, he believes my words. The Word of God clearly tells us how to claim and possess all that our Father wants us to have. So, why should anyone have trouble taking our Heavenly

Father God at His Word? If we walk in innocence, we accept everything without question. Innocence often unknowingly steps into that dominion.

My oldest son, Calvin, wants to preach like me and dress like me. When I gave away one of my favorite suits to a pastor, he took his favorite suit and gave it to the pastor's son. In imitating me, he discovered that the act of sowing allowed him to reap something greater. He knows he can trust my example. Innocence learns to grab hold of things that are more powerful. When we got our new van, he ran around the neighborhood telling everyone to come see his new van. He didn't work for or pay for the van, but it was his daddy's, so he claimed it as his own. Only a heart of innocence can do that.

Receiving Innocence

Then He took a little *child* and set him in the midst of them. And when He had taken him in His arms, He said to them,

"Whoever receives one of these little children in My name receives Me; and whoever receives Me, receives not Me but Him who sent Me."

Mark 9:36-37

So how does God want us to view each other? He wants us to see each other as little children. Always keep things in the perspective of innocence. So often, when we deal with children, we are dealing with innocence.

Jesus told the disciples "when you have seen Me, then you have seen My Father which is in heaven" (John 14:9). We are to be just like our Daddy God. Everything He can do, we can do. Our Father walks on water. Our Father tells the winds and the waves to be still. Our Father raises the dead. As our example, Jesus is showing us that when others see us, they should be seeing our Father. Jesus put a strong emphasis on walking in the innocence of a child and receiving things as a child. What stops us from being just like our Father? The loss of innocence. A lot of preachers are powerful speakers, but they can't walk on water or raise the dead because they have lost their innocence.

Then they brought young *children* to Him, that He might touch them; but the disciples rebuked those who brought them.

But when Jesus saw it, He was greatly displeased and said to them, "Let the little children come to Me, and do not forbid them; for of such is the kingdom of God.

"Assuredly, I say to you, whoever does not receive the kingdom of God as a little child will by no means enter it."

And He took them up in His arms, put His hands on them, and blessed them.

Mark 10:13-16

Then, what is the Kingdom of God? It is like the innocence of little children. What did God say concerning faith? He said to have faith as a little child. What is a child's faith? It is absolute trust in the one who is his security. A little child doesn't doubt that everything his Daddy says is true. For instance, if I tell my little boy that he can have a motorbike, he knows I will buy him one because I keep my word. Why does God say only those like little children will enter the kingdom of God? Because it is easy for a child to believe that whatever his Daddy says is going to happen will happen. If his Daddy says he is healed, then he is healed. Whatever his Daddy says, a child simply and innocently believes, therefore he can receive.

..."Assuredly, I say to you, unless you are converted and become as little children, you will by no means enter the kingdom of heaven."

Matthew 18:3

At that time Jesus answered and said, "I thank You, Father, Lord of heaven and earth, because You have hidden these things from the wise and prudent and have revealed them to babes.

"Even so, Father, for so it seemed good in Your sight."

Matthew 11:25,26

The Bible says you cannot enter the kingdom of God, unless you enter it like a child. Innocence will want to possess everything it can. When Calvin was a baby he would run around in his walker grabbing everything he could reach. He wanted to possess everything. Imagine if we were like that with our heavenly Father. Think what it would be like to go around heaven as a child. It would make your heavenly Father so happy. He might block some things that He knows you aren't ready to handle, but He would let you enjoy every good gift. You see innocence has no problem claiming everything that is the Father's. That includes omniscience and omnipresence. He has blessed us with every spiritual blessing in heavenly places in Christ.

Blessed be the God and Father of our Lord Jesus Christ, who has blessed us with every spiritual blessing in the heavenly places in Christ.

Ephesians 1:3

Someone who walks in innocence knows that in Christ, everything belonging to Dad is also his. Innocence has no problem claiming every spiritual blessing in heavenly places in Christ.

Mark 10:15 says if you don't receive the Kingdom of God as a child, you will not enter it at all. How does a child enter the Kingdom of God? He enters it with innocence.

Innocence is unimpaired integrity. Because of this, innocence can claim all rights to the power of God. The only thing that can hold back innocence is iniquity.

Iniquity will cause us to bend and miss the mark as an arrow that is shot at a target. Iniquity damages integrity.

Like arrows in the hand of a warrior, so are the children of one's youth.

Happy is the man who has his quiver full of them; they shall not be ashamed, but shall speak with their enemies in the gate.

Psalm 127:4,5

When an arrow is made, the craftsman picks a branch that is bent. He strips the branch of all bark and lays it in a groove to soak in water until it is pliable. Once it is pliable, it is put into a vice grip until it dries straight. Once it is straight, the tip can be applied and it is ready to hit its intended target.

Just like an arrow, the water of the Word will make you pliable by removing the iniquity. The discipline of the Holy Spirit's direction will bring the necessary submission and authority to "straighten" you. Once submission is reached innocence can then be restored.

Have the workers of iniquity no knowledge, who eat up my people as they eat bread, and do not call upon God?

Psalm 53:4

✼ "Iniquity" means [1]*crookedness, perverseness*, i.e. *evil regarded as that which is not straight or upright, moral distortion* (from the word `iwwah, *to bend, make crooked, pervert*).

Why is it that so often when we get close to what we want something inside us keeps of us from getting it? Too often Christians can't see the image of what belongs to them because they have received patterns or images from the enemy that cloud them from looking through the eyes of innocence. What is the Kingdom of God? Little children coming and possessing all that is their Father's. Without a doubt, everything that Daddy has is mine. Whatever my Daddy God says, I can believe. Are we accepting the price Jesus paid for us? First Peter 2:24 says, "By his stripes, we were healed," but when we go for our healing, sin stops us from receiving the promises of our Father. Why? It is because we must first understand that iniquity is out to keep us from maintaining the innocence to grasp our sonship with God. The devil knows that if we approach God as innocently as a child does, we can have everything we lay claim to.

Receiving Sonship

Now I say that the heir, as long as he is a child, does not differ at all from a slave, though he is master of all,

but is under guardians and stewards until the time appointed by the father.

Even so we, when we were children, were in bondage under the elements of the world.

But when the fullness of the time had come, God sent forth His Son, born of a woman, born under the law,

to redeem those who were under the law, that we might receive the adoption as sons.

And because you are sons, God has sent forth the Spirit of His Son into your hearts, crying out, "Abba, Father!"

Therefore you are no longer a slave but a son, and if a son, then an heir of God through Christ.

Galatians 4:1-7

Don't ever lose the awe of God being your Father. Innocence has no problem understanding that God is Daddy and Father. The fourth chapter of Galatians reveals the Christian who understands innocence. From the beginning of this chapter, it speaks of a child moving into sonship. Through the entire process, innocence is never lost. God never intended innocence to be lost to anyone.

Chapter 2

Defining Innocence

Enjoyment — Leaving Nothing to Ask

In the Daniel Webster's 1828 Dictionary, innocence is described as:

Properly, freedom from any quality that can injure harmlessness.

Take my youngest son, Christopher, who is less than a year old. He is free from any quality that can injure harmlessness. He has no sense of what can cause him harm because he is innocent. Webster's definition goes on to say:

In a moral sense, freedom from crime, sin or guilt; untainted purity of heart and life; unimpaired integrity.

How much of a child's integrity is damaged at a young age? Maybe more than you might think. The devil is out to destroy innocence. He does not want us to come into the innocence God desires for us. The devil certainly doesn't want the restoration of innocence in the body of Christ so that we are walking in the full power of God. We need to restore and guard innocence in the body of Christ because it carries a purity of power.

Dr. Samuel Johnson 1700's Dictionary defines innocence as:

Freedom from guilt or intentions, simplicity of heart as the innocence of a child.

Have you ever noticed how children are so free with their happiness? They have so many things to enjoy it leaves little for them to ask for. A small child fears nothing. The only way his integrity is impaired or his innocence is damaged is if he is taught fear. If my son Calvin, who is 7, sees that I am afraid of something, then he is likely to be afraid of the same thing. By doing so, I impair his integrity and innocence. I begin to strip him of innocence and power when I allow him to experience fear.

Many people are totally unaware of how innocence is destroyed. Most parents begin to destroy innocence in their children at a very young age without a clue about what they are doing. Remember, the goal of the devil is to destroy innocence. Even some of ministers whose homes I have been in think it is okay for children to watch certain movies just because they are widely accepted as being okay for children.

For example, I had a little boy come to me one day and begin to cry. He was about four years old. I asked him what was wrong. He told me that his mother had gone on a trip for four days and he was afraid she was going to die because he had watched an "innocent" movie made for children where the mother of this baby deer died. I didn't know much about this movie so I began to check it out. It is rated G. But when a child's story builds fear into children, you have to ask yourself if it is of God. The devil's strategy is to build images of fear in us to keep us from receiving God's images. What good roots to launch so called purity and simplicity in a movie? It is G-Rated, nothing naked or vulgar.

This same company produced another very popular movie where the main characters were lions. It is about a young lion as his dead predecessors lead him through life. That is nothing more than witchcraft. Many Christians believe it is harmless for their children, but is it? It depends upon our standard and scale and where we believe God wants to take us. Does it breed God's creativity in them? Or does it keep them from walking in the purity of God?

Isn't our Christianity watered down by the influence of the American way of life? We are now seeing Christian-based movies that allow us to empathize instead of being moved with God's compassion. We bought our little boy a Christian video; once we watched this video we found out that this movie exalts the deafness of a young boy. It doesn't move us to want the deaf ears opened by the power of God. It teaches us to accept the way things are. It opens no doors for this boy to tap into God's creative power and be healed. These movies are substitutes that Satan uses to rob people of God's creative power by not moving in innocence towards the things God desires.

When I took my son Calvin to a popular fast food restaurant he received a toy from the movie, *The Hunchback of Notre Dame*. When he opened it and saw this poor deformed man, he began to cry. I asked him what was the matter and he replied, "This man needs to be healed." That is what I mean when I say we cannot teach our children to accept things the way they are. If we accept things the way they are then we will never be moved to compassion, to see blind eyes opened or deaf ears hearing as God wants us to.

In America today there are churches that draw the teenage population in by fantasy, manipulation, lust and pornography. You think that isn't happening. Many Christian youth centers have pinball machines with scantily clad girls that only offer games with murder and violence in them, then sit them down, and teach them the Word. Is it any wonder why these teens are not able to grow into strong Christians? We need to teach our children to have a power base experience in God's reality not in mindless fantasies. The devil will always create a substitute for the real power if we are willing to fall for his gimmicks.

When we try to use the world's system to get people saved, we are treading on volatile ground destroying innocence. There are those who think our youth centers have to be filled with violent video games to bring people to God. Many churches today use the world's system to get people saved. Do we think we are going to get our children on fire for God like that? Children need to see the real power of God.

Time after time, I have prayed for people that were unable to receive the power of God. I would try so hard to get them to step into the supernatural. Somewhere inside of them are images that had been ingrained in their conscience that they haven't known or chosen to allow the blood of Christ to wash. They couldn't understand what kept them from moving into God's creative power or seeing the supernatural. Remember that purity equals power.

If you want your child to step into the supernatural and be able to contain and release the fullness of the power of God, you have to eliminate those things that will destroy his innocence towards God. Fear destroys a person's ability to innocently come to God. Faith believes God for everything.

I see lots of evangelists and ministers from other countries that are so full of the power of God. I believe it is because they did not grow up with a continual bombardment of the corruption than this society holds — television being the worst offender. These ministers had less manipulations, controls and fantasies to wear away at their innocence. Their visions and images aren't as damaged as those who grow up in nations where news and entertainment are a dominant way of life. The United States stands as a prime example of how Satan's influences masquerade the Egyptian system that has continually worn away at the conscious innocence of a country. The people who are raised with their senses dulled stand in bewilderment when we move with power.

Innocence and Focus

The Bible says that for the joy that was set before Him, Jesus endured the cross (Hebrews 12:2). He was absolutely focused on His goal; although the devil was trying everything he could to distract Jesus from that focus. The devil will do whatever he can to hinder you from getting where God wants you to go. He will throw up roadblocks, obstacles, false images and wayward ideas before you. That doesn't mean you will not have a vision that is out of this world. You may believe it is God's plan for your life, but it is an Ishmael vision, not the Isaac vision that is God's best. An Ishmael vision is a substitute for the real thing. Isaac was the son God called Abraham and Sarah to have, but they couldn't wait for the vision to come to pass, they decided to bring the vision to pass on their own, thus bringing an Ishmael vision to pass. When integrity and innocence have been impaired or destroyed, so has your clarity for the perfect vision God wants for you.

15

My oldest boy is a little different since he began visiting in people's homes where they do not understand how to guard innocence. The barriers of his innocence have been attacked, but this does not mean that his innocence has been lost or destroyed. What is lost can be restored. As parents, we need to guard against demonic invasion into the innocent lives of our children. We need to be careful to protect the pure innocence in them. Children can readily accept the fact that all our Father has is theirs too. Innocence has no problem claiming what belongs to it. Innocence enjoys without asking. Children accept without question. That is what innocence is.

Don't your children have free access to what belongs to your household? Don't you think it is the same with our heavenly Father? Think about it. Somewhere along the way, we have learned to be afraid. The devil has robbed us of innocence by building fear, doubt, unbelief and insecurity within us. He keeps us from a strong relationship with our Father where we are no longer afraid to receive the blessings that are freely given to us.

In America today television is so popular that the first thing people do to babies when they are born is place them in front of it and leave them there for hours on end. The devil has a system of fear developing in children almost from the day they are born. He has people deceived into believing that cartoons are safe because they are animated. Most cartoons have more violence than shows made for adults. Yet, this is what we place before our innocent children to entertain them. The devil begins to slowly destroy their innocence with cartoons and video games until there is none left. Some of the video games that my son played at friends' homes caused him to have nightmares later. After waking him from the nightmare, we'd find out how the fear came in when we prayed for him.

Innocence Has No Fear

There was an incredible work of innocence in David when he was young. He played his harp to the Lord God out of pure love. Then, one day he goes out to the battlefield and sees everyone is afraid of a giant named Goliath. In the midst of David's innocence, he doesn't think twice about killing Goliath. After all, he is an uncircumcised Philistine! He is wicked and David stands righteous before God. In David's mind, he can only win! Think about how he is thinking. There is a purity flowing through him. He is not a warrior. He is a psalmist who has no fear. Purity possesses great power. How did God judge David the day he came against Goliath?

His brothers were older than he was but they were cowards. They got angry when David showed up because his motives were pure and his brothers' fear of Goliath caused them great embarrassment. But David ignored their responses. He knew what his heavenly Father could do. After all, God had delivered him from the lion and the bear while he tended his father's sheep. Who was this uncircumcised Philistine to think himself different? In David's innocence, he knew his Daddy had no problem taking out the devil no matter what form he came in.

From the beginning of time, the devil did not want this type of innocence to come into the world. He launched a full-scale attack. He knew fear would make people unable to fight or defend themselves. He works hard at developing his weapon of fear in people.

Chapter 3
The Work of Innocence

Innocence Establishes A Throne

"**N**ow if you walk before Me as your father David walked, in integrity [or innocence] of heart and in uprightness, to do according to all that I have commanded you, and if you keep My statutes and My judgments,

"then I will establish the throne of your kingdom over Israel forever, as I promised David your father, saying, 'You shall not fail to have a man on the throne of Israel.'

1 King 9:4,5

God decided to establish a throne forever through King David (2 Samuel 7:12,13). Why did He choose David? He based it on the innocence of David's heart. If you walk in innocence God will set up a throne forever.

Innocence of heart will establish the throne, the destiny and the greatest empowerment God has for you. To maintain innocence, you have to guard yourself from bitterness, unforgiveness, anger, strife, hurt and pain. It is coming to a place of no offense. That means when you are attacked, you don't attack back. You are actually taking a continual stance in the realm of the spirit. It is as though you are saying "yes" to God handling your

19

affairs and "no" to any unrenewed flesh that keeps you from looking to your Father for every provision. Innocence will always bring and work restoration.

Innocence Brings Restoration

Then the LORD said to Satan, "Have you considered My servant Job, that there is none like him on the earth, a blameless and upright man, one who fears God and shuns evil? And still he holds fast to his integrity, although you incited Me against him, to destroy him without cause."

Job 1:8

Do you want to know what restored Job's life? It was his innocence. As long as Job continued to walk in innocence and purity of heart, he could find atonement. Job continually prayed for his children out of innocence just in case they were sinning. He held fast to innocence. He loved God.

Then his wife said to him, "Do you still hold fast to your integrity? Curse God and die!"

Job 2:9

But Job stayed in a place of simplicity. He knew God was always there. There was a unique innate trust moving from Job towards God. In this entire process there is an incredible form of deliverance and restoration in the making.

Let me be weighed on honest scales, that God may know my integrity.

Job 31:6

Job asked God to weigh him on honest scales that he would hold onto his innocence. Everyone is weighed to determine his or her innocence.

All a man's ways seem innocent to him, but motives are weighed by the LORD.

Proverbs 16:2 (NIV)

When innocence is fed with love, it does not think twice about trusting.

Though He slay me, yet will I trust Him....

Job 13:15

Trusting comes automatically. When I love my boys, trusting comes automatically. They trust that dad will do what he says because he loves! So, in a sense one has to find the innocence of the Lord in somebody and feed it with love.

When I first came to America, I was part of a youth group that went out witnessing on the street. One night we led a young man to the Lord. The next week the whole group of us started to go to a movie together. As we climbed out of the car and walk to the theater, I heard the Lord speak the scripture to me that Jesus spoke to the Pharisees. "You go around the whole world to win one convert to make him twice a son of hell as you are." I froze in the middle of my steps thinking, "What in the world am I doing?" Here was this young man that we just led to the Lord a week ago and we are teaching him to compromise with the world.

My conscience was seared. I no longer had the innocence that I once had. I allowed compromise to creep in and rob my innocence. Compromise breeds compromise. It has taken me a lot of tears and a lot of time on my knees to find out what it is like to trust as a child and to have that innocence restored within me. Of course, I am a man but each one of us needs the innocence of a child within our heart when trusting God.

21

The same thing happened again when I began dating my wife. I took her to see a movie that I thought was innocent. When I picked her up at her apartment, she had no television. Her great grandfather was a Nazarene Evangelist, a holiness preacher, very pure and she was taught those ways from childhood.

In the movie, someone was murdered. Tears started rolling down her face. I looked at her and she had her eyes covered crying. I asked her what was wrong. She said, "I can't stand this. I never watch this kind of stuff." I got up and walked out in the lobby and asked the Holy Spirit what I was doing wrong. He said to me, "You are searing her conscience." I was exposing her to accept evil in her heart.

My son has a Christian video called Bible Man. In the video, you shoot the enemy with verses. But it teaches him the Word, because he has already been exposed to the Word so it can be continually worked in him through this video. But my younger son Daniel runs and hides when he sees this video playing. I have seen him do that several times with a lot of different videos, where there was some type of violence including word for word the book of Matthew, where Jesus is being crucified. I realized there was something in his spirit that is grieved. His innocence has never been compromised, so therefore it was uncomfortable and frightning to him.

Innocence and Intimacy with God

In Hebrew one of the expressions of intimacy is "stroking the face," which shows a picture of the Father stroking His son's face. Have you ever seen a mother stroke her baby's face? It is an expression of her love for that child.

> **Since you were precious in My sight, you have been honored, and I have loved you; therefore I will give men for you, and people for your life.**
>
> **Isaiah 43:4**

In this scripture, I can see my Father God stroking my face. It is His way of saying how precious I am to Him. He says, "I love you so much." It is just as a mother would do for her child. Why can't we have the simplicity of heart to say, "I want to get into my Daddy's shoes?"

Innocence Will Preserve You

> **Let integrity and uprightness preserve me, for I wait for You.**
>
> **Psalm 25:21**

> **The way of a guilty man is devious, but the conduct of the innocent is upright.**
>
> **Proverbs 21:8 (NIV)**

Innocence will preserve you. In the Bible, the word that is interpreted "integrity" is "tummah." It can also be interpreted as "innocence". It means *completeness; figuratively, prosperity; usually (morally) innocence: full, integrity, perfect (-ion), simplicity, upright (-ly, -ness), at a venture.* The word "tummah" is pronounced "toomaw". Remember, in the following scriptures, the word for "integrity" could also be translated "innocence."

> **Vindicate me, O LORD, for I have walked in my integrity [innocence]. I have also trusted in the LORD; I shall not slip.**
>
> **Psalm 26:1**

> **But as for me, I will walk in my integrity [innocence]; redeem me and be merciful to me.**
>
> **Psalm 26:11**

Out of a relationship of integrity with God, he was saying he knew he could trust his heavenly Daddy to listen and act on his behalf because God knew his heart.

The integrity [innocence] *of the upright* **will guide them, but the perversity of the unfaithful will destroy them.**

Proverbs 11:3

A person of innocence knows if he goes into a place of danger there is no need to fear. An innocent person has the power inside him to overcome all fears and obstacles. Why? Because he is upright before God. One way to begin to restore integrity and innocence in a righteous person is by overcoming fear through love and faith. When we overcome fear, we can restore our innocence.

⚒ When innocence is fed with love, it does not think twice about trusting. Trusting comes automatically. As I show love to my boys, they automatically trust me. They trust that dad will do what he says because he loves them so much! When my boy, Daniel, says, "Catch me, daddy," he is really saying, "I trust you to catch me, daddy." He totally believes I am not going to let him fall. Although I am imperfect, I could never let this trusting little boy fall. How much more our Heavenly Father has all we need to keep us steadfast in every situation.

And He will establish you to the end [keep you steadfast, give you strength, and guarantee your vindication: He will be your warrant against all accusation or indictment so that you will be] guiltless and irreproachable in the day of our Lord Jesus Christ, (the Messiah).

God is faithful (reliable, trustworthy, and therefore, Ever true to His promise, and He can be depended on): By Him you were called into com-

panionship and Participation with His Son, Jesus Christ, our Lord.

1 Corinthians 1:8,9 (AMP)

So, in a sense, you restore innocence in somebody by feeding him God's love. It has taken me a lot of tears and time on my knees to find out what it is like to trust as a child.

Innocence Brings Blessing

The righteous man walks in his integrity [innocence]; his children are blessed after him.

Proverbs 20:7

When you sow innocence in a child, you are sowing great blessings for him. You are teaching him to be an overcomer. Blessings follow the man who walks in innocence. Teach your children about the power of purity and you will see great rewards. *The innocence of the upright opens doors to great blessings.*

When my little boy sees me loving and putting my trust in God, it builds that same trust in him. I remember a meeting where the power of God was dramatically touching people. Near the end of the service, I prayed for Calvin, anointing him all over with oil. The anointing was so strong he began to shake under the power of God. His entire body was so red it looked like he was on fire. I picked him up and held him while he prayed for a lady. The Holy Spirit told me to leave him alone and let him pray for the people. Everyone he touched fell out under the power of God. Some people said that wherever he touched them, it felt like a handprint of fire on that spot.

Later that night, Calvin said, "Daddy, I saw Jesus holding my hand. I knew when I touched people demons would leave. I saw three angels acting as ushers

25

when I prayed for people. I didn't want to let go of Jesus' hand."

That conversation touched me because I knew he couldn't have gotten that from anything anyone had said. He doesn't know what I know. He hasn't studied as I have. The power of innocence is strong.

Innocence Through Covenant

Some people may argue they are innocent by the blood. But Paul said not to sin just because grace abounds (Romans 6:1). Through the blood covenant, we are given the power and ability to walk in innocence.

And according to the law almost all things are purified with blood, and without shedding of blood there is no remission.

Hebrews 9:22

And do not present your members as instruments of unrighteousness to sin, but present yourselves to God as being alive from the dead, and your members as instruments of righteousness to God.

For sin shall not have dominion over you, for you are not under law but under grace.

What then? Shall we sin because we are not under law but under grace? Certainly not!

Do you not know that to whom you present yourselves slaves to obey, you are that one's slaves whom you obey, whether of sin leading to death, or of obedience leading to righteousness?

Romans 6:13-16

The word "righteousness" in the last verse is the word "dikaiosune." This word is from the root word "dikaios," which means; *equitable (in character or act); by implication, innocent, holy (absolutely or relatively).*

But God be thanked that though you were slaves of sin, yet you obeyed from the heart that form of doctrine to which you were delivered.

And having been set free from sin, you became slaves of righteousness.

I speak in human terms because of the weakness of your flesh. For just as you presented your members as slaves of uncleanness, and of lawlessness leading to more lawlessness, so now present your members as slaves of righteousness for holiness.

Romans 6:17-19

The word holiness is "hagiasmos"; *purification, i.e. (the state) purity; concretely (by Hebraism) a purifier: holiness, sanctification.*

Through the blood of Jesus, we have been given the ability to walk in innocence. But the devil has deceived people into thinking that they can live the ways of the world during the week and run to the altar on Sunday to repent and go back to the world again on Monday. This is not innocence. This is exactly what Paul is talking about in these verses in Romans 6:17-19. Grace does not give us the "right" to sin because we have the ability to repent. James 4:17 says, "Therefore, to him who knows to do good and does not do it, to him it is sin."

for the wrath of man does not produce the righteousness of God.

Therefore lay aside all filthiness and overflow of wickedness, and receive with meekness the implanted word, which is able to save your souls.

But be doers of the word, and not hearers only, deceiving yourselves.

James 1:20-22

Job 31:1-40 gives us a Biblical definition of innocence:

"I have made a covenant with my eyes; why then should I look upon a young woman?

For what is the allotment of God from above, and the inheritance of the Almighty from on high?

Is it not destruction for the wicked, and disaster for the workers of iniquity?

Does He not see my ways, and count all my steps?

If I have walked with falsehood, or if my foot has hastened to deceit,

Let me be weighed on honest scales, that God may know my integrity [innocence].

If my step has turned from the way, or my heart walked after my eyes, or if any spot adheres to my hands,

Then let me sow, and another eat; yes, let my harvest be rooted out.

"If my heart has been enticed by a woman, or if I have lurked at my neighbor's door,

Then let my wife grind for another, and let others bow down over her.

For that would be wickedness; yes, it would be iniquity deserving of judgment.

For that would be a fire that consumes to destruction, and would root out all my increase.

"If I have despised the cause of my male or female servant when they complained against me,

What then shall I do when God rises up? When He punishes, how shall I answer Him?

Did not He who made me in the womb make them? Did not the same One fashion us in the womb?

"If I have kept the poor from their desire, or caused the eyes of the widow to fail,

Or eaten my morsel by myself, so that the fatherless may not eat of it

(But from my youth I reared him as a father, and from my mother's womb I guided the widow);

If I have seen anyone perish for lack of clothing, or any poor man without covering;

If his heart has not blessed me, and if he was not warmed with the fleece of my sheep;

If I have raised my hand against the fatherless, when I saw I had help in the gate;

Then let my arm fall from my shoulder, let my arm be torn from the socket.

For destruction from God is a terror to me, and because of His magnificence I could not endure.

"If I have made gold my hope, or said to fine gold, 'You are my confidence';

If I have rejoiced because my wealth was great, and because my hand had gained much;

If I have observed the sun when it shines, or the moon moving in brightness,

So that my heart has been secretly enticed, and my mouth has kissed my hand;

This also would be an iniquity worthy of judgment, for I would have denied God who is above.

"If I have rejoiced at the destruction of him who hated me, or lifted myself up when evil found him

(Indeed I have not allowed my mouth to sin by asking for a curse on his soul);

If the men of my tent have not said, 'Who is there that has not been satisfied with his meat?'

(But no sojourner had to lodge in the street, for I have opened my doors to the traveler);

If I have covered my transgressions as Adam, by hiding my iniquity in my bosom,

Because I feared the great multitude, and dreaded the contempt of families, so that I kept silence and did not go out of the door—

Oh, that I had one to hear me! Here is my mark. Oh, that the Almighty would answer me, that my Prosecutor had written a book!

Surely I would carry it on my shoulder, and bind it on me like a crown;

I would declare to Him the number of my steps; like a prince I would approach Him.

"If my land cries out against me, and its furrows weep together;

If I have eaten its fruit without money, or caused its owners to lose their lives;

Then let thistles grow instead of wheat, and weeds instead of barley." The words of Job are ended.

Job 31:1-40

The Weight of Innocence

Let me be weighed on honest scales, that God may know my integrity [innocence].

Job 31:6

Job kept coming back to the root of what he knew was the purest thing between God and him — his innocence. He knew if his Father God examined their relationship, He would know Job's desire was to be just like Him. God is coming back to examine our hearts to see if our relationship with Him is like a child with his Father. Job said God would weigh innocence (verse 6). In the book of Daniel, Belshazzar's innocence was weighed and found to be lacking. What was the result?

"TEKEL: You have been weighed in the balances, and found wanting;

"PERES: Your kingdom has been divided, and given to the Medes and Persians."

That very night Belshazzar, king of the Chaldeans, was slain.

Daniel 5:27-28, 30

God desires innocence. Those who are lack innocence will not escape the eyes of God.

Chapter 4

The Destruction of Innocence

Therefore be as shrewd as snakes and as innocent as doves.

Matthew 10:16 (NIV)

The devil's goal has always been to destroy innocence. From the beginning of time he knew that a deliverer would come to tear down his kingdom, so he set
out to destroy him. The only problem was he didn't
know who his destroyer would be, so he had to attack
many children to be sure he got the right one.

**And he [Pharaoh] said to his people, "Look, the
people of the children of Israel are more and
mightier than we;**

**"Come, let us deal shrewdly with them, lest
they multiply, and it happen, in the event of war,
that they also join our enemies and fight against
us, and so go up out of the land."**

**Therefore they set taskmasters over them to
afflict them with their burdens. And they built
for Pharaoh supply cities, Pithom and Raamses.**

**But the more they afflicted them, the more they
multiplied and grew. And they were in dread of
the children of Israel.**

So the Egyptians made the children of Israel serve with rigor.

And they made their lives bitter with hard bondage— in mortar, in brick, and in all manner of service in the field. All their service in which they made them serve was with rigor.

Exodus 1:9-14

So Pharaoh commanded all his people, saying, "Every son who is born you shall cast into the river, and every daughter you shall save alive."

Exodus 1:22

Moreover He said, "I am the God of your father— the God of Abraham, the God of Isaac, and the God of Jacob." And Moses hid his face, for he was afraid to look upon God.

And the LORD said: "I have surely seen the oppression of My people who are in Egypt, and have heard their cry because of their taskmasters, for I know their sorrows.

Exodus 3:6,7

"Now therefore, behold, the cry of the children of Israel has come to Me, and I have also seen the oppression with which the Egyptians oppress them.

"Come now, therefore, and I will send you to Pharaoh that you may bring My people, the children of Israel, out of Egypt."

Exodus 3:9,10

As time passed, Satan knew that the true deliverer was near. Once again, he tried to eliminate him by destroying the children. This time he was after Jesus.

Now after Jesus was born in Bethlehem of Judea in the days of Herod the king, behold, wise men from the East came to Jerusalem, saying, "Where is He who has been born King of the Jews? For we have seen His star in the East and have come to worship Him."

When Herod the king heard this, he was troubled, and all Jerusalem with him.

Matthew 2:1,3

Then Herod, when he had secretly called the wise men, determined from them what time the star appeared.

And he sent them to Bethlehem and said, "Go and search diligently for the young Child, and when you have found Him, bring back word to me, that I may come and worship Him also."

Matthew 2:7,8

Then, being divinely warned in a dream that they should not return to Herod, they departed for their own country another way.

Matthew 2:12

Then Herod, when he saw that he was deceived by the wise men, was exceedingly angry; and he sent forth and put to death all the male children who were in Bethlehem and in all its districts, from two years old and under, according to the time which he had determined from the wise men.

Matthew 2:16

The devil knows that the key to destroying innocence is by eliminating the innocence of children. A child is innocent until something comes in to destroy that innocence. A child will believe anything he is told.

If you told a two-year-old boy he is going to become a king, he would believe it. So the devil's plan was to get rid of anyone two years and under to be sure no one could believe he was going to become a king.

Innocence is a key to defying death. Do you know why? Because our Father possesses life and those, who will innocently believe in Him can defy death. Jesus took the keys to death, hell and the grave. The last enemy to be put beneath your feet is death. When you are innocent, you can possess life. An innocent child has no concept of aging. All he can see is the excitement of life right now. An innocent child has no concept of yielding to disease or infirmity.

Innocence is the key to defying everything that manipulates and controls us today. Innocence will break the barriers of manipulation, control, false images and wrong visions. We need to get a clear picture of how the blood of Christ purges our conscience of all dead works if we want to restore innocence within us.

Isn't it amazing how a child doesn't wonder where his next meal is coming from? How much more will God care for us? Why do we worry? Doesn't He clothe the lilies of the field that are greater than Solomon's splendor (Matthew 6:28,29)? In innocence, you won't wonder whether God is going to take care of you or not. In your innocence, you can expect care. You can know that all your needs will be met.

If ye then, being evil, know how to give good gifts unto your children, how much more shall your Father which is in heaven give good things to them that ask him?
Matthew 7:11

My son, Daniel, is very young. He has no concept of not having a need met. It is so easy to see this in a child. Yet, when it comes to trusting our Father, we wonder whether He will meet our needs or not. How much more is God able to meet our needs than we are able to take care of our own children?

God's desire is to build an unlimited vision of His potential within each of us. If we can have the innocence of a child, we will begin to see so powerfully in the spirit. The purity of mind and heart lays a pattern and foundation for God to establish His dreams and visions within each of us. The pure in heart will see God (Matthew 5:8).

God amazes me with what my little boy sees. One day in the front room he said, "Dad, it's raining all around you". I said, "No, son, it's not. I'm in the house." He said, "But it's raining little drops of gold". I said, "Thank you, I receive that!"

The devil brings in his own images in an attempt to destroy the pure images God intends for us to have. A good example of this is what happened to me as a small boy growing up in South Africa. We did not have televisions, so for after-school entertainment, they would show us reel-to-reel movies brought in from overseas. But my dad always told me to come right home after school. One day I rebelled and went to see the movie anyway. I knew he was working late, so I figured I could watch *Dracula* and get home without him knowing that I watched it.

Many years later, a group of us went to this church where a funeral was being held. We had two hours before the funeral to "practice" raising this lady from the dead. When we laid hands on her, her eyes started moving. That is when I freaked and ran out of the church. The first thing that came to my mind was the picture of *Dracula* coming alive. That movie put an image of fear in my mind, which kept us from raising a lady from the dead. Since that experience, I rebuked that fear and have become overwhelmed with God's love to bring life. Now that I am walking in innocence, we have seen several raised from the dead.

Chapter 5

Rebellion Destroys Innocence

Those who walk in innocence have no problem believing God. When my little boy, Calvin, sees me wave my hand and people fall under the power of God, he easily does the same thing. When I anoint him and pray over him, he can run all over the auditorium praying for people. They will fall under the power of God because of his innocent belief in God's power.

Are all children innocent? Yes, until parents unwittingly allow ungodly relationships, video games and television rebellion to plant fears and demonic ideas in them. It robs them of the innocence God needs for His work to be done through them. Watch over your children carefully when they are with you. Pray for laborers to come before your children when they are in the wrong environment where Satan's influence is strong. It is vital that we put a stop to rebellion when we see it.

King David was a man who had integrity and innocence of heart. He walked before the Lord in innocence all the days of his life. The following prayer by David reveals the motives of the enemy, but also the motives of his own godly heart.

Hear my voice, O God, in my meditation; preserve my life from fear of the enemy.

Hide me from the secret plots of the wicked, from the rebellion of the workers of iniquity,

Who sharpen their tongue like a sword, and bend their bows to shoot their arrows — bitter words,

That they may shoot in secret at the blameless; suddenly they shoot at him and do not fear.

They encourage themselves in an evil matter; they talk of laying snares secretly; they say, "Who will see them?"

They devise iniquities: "We have perfected a shrewd scheme." Both the inward thought and the heart of man are deep.

But God shall shoot at them with an arrow; suddenly they shall be wounded.

So He will make them stumble over their own tongue; all who see them shall flee away.

All men shall fear, and shall declare the work of God; for they shall wisely consider His doing.

The righteous shall be glad in the LORD, and trust in Him. And all the upright in heart shall glory.

Psalm 64:1-10

At the end of this chapter, we see David encouraged himself by saying, "the upright or the innocent in heart shall glory." Satan did all he could to maneuver David outside the realm of innocence, but David was able to remain innocent in heart. Through all his life experiences, He did not allow rebellion to take root and overtake his heart.

Surely (behold) I have behaved and quieted myself (my soul), as a child that is weaned of his mother: my soul is even as a weaned child
Psalm 131:2

The devil's goal is to maneuver a person outside the place of innocence and into the place of rebellion. When you can no longer clearly see that all the heavenly Father has belongs to you, you are no longer able to believe you have every right to possess it. Rebellion breeds a vision of fear, doubt and unbelief. If your perception to believe is clouded, you are unable to receive.

For instance, our Father owns the cattle on a thousand hills (Psalm 50:10). Our Daddy is rich. If you have a need — He has *no problem* in meeting it. Can you believe it? Or have false poverty doctrines and other deceptive philosophies and man-made traditions destroyed your innocently accepting this truth?

⚹ Religious demons destroy innocence. Yet, those possessing religious demons couldn't intimidate Stephen in Acts Chapter 7:2-53. He told them they had killed the righteous One without fear of what they would do to Him. He boldly reminded them of how they killed the prophets who were sent to them by God and now they had killed the only One, the Messiah, whom God had sent to save them from all their sin.

Here you see a man who wasn't afraid. His face shone with the glory of God because he was fully innocence to the death. When they stoned him, he stayed innocent. He asked God not to hold their sin against them. Innocence doesn't get offended, angry, or bitter. Innocence has no anxiety, worry, confusion or doubt. An innocent man knows God has everything under control regardless of any situation he faces.

41

Chapter 6
Innocence Protects

The LORD shall judge the peoples; judge me,
O LORD, according to my righteousness, and
according to my integrity [innocence] within me.

Psalm 7:8

In this Scripture, David wants God to judge him
according to his innocence. That is a bold statement.
David based his statement on his relationship and
understanding of God's ability to see him as he really
was. He trusted God to know the intimacy of their relationship. He knew God could see that in his heart he
was as an innocent child.

Look at this same principle at work in Genesis
chapter 20.

**And Abraham journeyed from there to the
South, and dwelt between Kadesh and Shur, and
stayed in Gerar.**

**Now Abraham said of Sarah his wife, "She is
my sister." And Abimelech king of Gerar sent and
took Sarah.**

**But God came to Abimelech in a dream by
night, and said to him, "Indeed you are a dead
man because of the woman whom you have
taken, for she is a man's wife."**

> But Abimelech had not come near her; and he said, "Lord, will You slay a righteous nation also?

> "Did he not say to me, 'She is my sister'? And she, even she herself said, 'He is my brother.' *In the integrity of my heart and innocence* of my hands I have done this."

> And God said to him in a dream, "Yes, I know that you did this in the integrity of your heart. For I also withheld you from sinning against Me; therefore I did not let you touch her.
>
> **Genesis 20:1-6**

In this passage, we see God guarding innocence. Here is a king who does not appear to believe in God, but God comes to him in a dream and protects him from sinning with Abraham's wife because the king acted in innocence. Abraham and Sarah both lied. They were wrong, yet God protected the innocence of this king. When God finds innocence in you, it brings out the nature of His divine protection. The king's heart was pure. Therefore, God offered Abimelech divine protection.

> "Now therefore, restore the man's wife; for he is a prophet, and he will pray for you and you shall live. But if you do not restore her, know that you shall surely die, you and all who are yours."
>
> **Genesis 20:7**

He listened to God. Innocence is powerful. God told him how to protect himself. After the king released Sarah to Abraham, the blessings began to flow. This is an important message for the body of Christ. If we want God to restore innocence within the church, we will need to guard our innocence. The devil wants us to stop us from *innocently* believing that God divinely protects us by His blood.

Little children, let no one deceive you. He who practices righteousness is righteous, just as He is righteous.

He who sins is of the devil, for the devil has sinned from the beginning. For this purpose the Son of God was manifested, that He might destroy the works of the devil.

1 John 3:7,8

But now in Christ Jesus you who once were far off have been brought near by the blood of Christ.

For He Himself is our peace, who has made both one, and has broken down the middle wall of separation,

Ephesians 2:13,14

In Him we have redemption through His blood, the forgiveness of sins, according to the riches of His grace

which He made to abound toward us in all wisdom and prudence,

Ephesians 1:7,8

Let no door be left open as the devil is looking for a way in.

Leave no [such] room or foothold for the devil [give no opportunity to him].

Ephesians 4:27 (AMP)

The devil knows those who possess innocence leave no door open for him to come through. There are many times we do not even protect the innocence of our own children. We cannot let the importance of innocence slip by us.

Chapter 7
Wash Your Hands in Innocence

Vindicate me, O LORD, for I have walked in my integrity [innocence]. I have also trusted in the LORD; I shall not slip.

Examine me, O LORD, and prove me; try my mind and my heart.

For Your lovingkindness is before my eyes, and I have walked in Your truth.

I have not sat with idolatrous mortals, nor will I go in with hypocrites.

I have hated the assembly of evildoers, and will not sit with the wicked.

I will wash my hands in innocence; so I will go about Your altar, O LORD,

Psalm 26:1-6

Another definition for innocence is unimpaired integrity. "I will wash my hands in innocence" (verse 6). Isn't it reassuring to lift your hands and know they are clean? I take hold of all that is my Dad's because God said that whatever a man puts his hands to do would prosper. I know I can take it freely because there is nothing in me that must suffer guilt, condemnation or shame. Without condemnation, you feel free to gain instant access to all the treasures of heaven.

Innocence is freedom from sin, guilt or fear. Innocence knows that whatever your heavenly Daddy gives you is good (James 1:17). Freely receive, freely give and in this you will see that the goodness of God that leads men to repentance (Romans 2:4).

When you are innocent, you accept His goodness. You will know how to show forth His goodness because His goodness lives in you. The power of your relationship with God is what draws people to want a relationship with God for themselves. You need to know your Father is with you holding your hand. This will help restore you to the place of innocence.

Yet the righteous will hold to his way, and he who has clean hands will be stronger and stronger.
Job 17:9

How will an innocent person know he is doing wrong? When one is innocent, he will have clean hands and a pure innocent heart. An innocent man will listen to his heart and his heart will tell him when he is doing wrong. God sees innocence. The following Scriptures describe the difference between a true believer and one who is not.

That I may proclaim with the voice of thanksgiving, and tell of all Your wondrous works.

LORD, I have loved the habitation of Your house, and the place where Your glory dwells.

Do not gather my soul with sinners, nor my life with bloodthirsty men,

In whose hands is a sinister scheme, and whose right hand is full of bribes.

But as for me, I will walk in my integrity [innocence]; redeem me and be merciful to me.

My foot stands in an even place; in the congregations I will bless the LORD.
Psalm 26:7-12

Chapter 8
The Question Is...
When Will We Return to Innocence?

"**S**et the trumpet to your mouth! He shall come like an eagle against the house of the LORD, because they have transgressed My covenant and rebelled against My law.

Israel will cry to Me, 'My God, we know You!'

Israel has rejected the good; the enemy will pursue him.

"They set up kings, but not by Me; they made princes, but I did not acknowledge them. From their silver and gold they made idols for themselves — that they might be cut off.

Your calf is rejected, O Samaria! My anger is aroused against them — *how long until they attain to innocence?*

For from Israel is even this: a workman made it, and it is not God; but the calf of Samaria shall be broken to pieces.

Hosea 8:1-6

Many people today are still building idols in their life. An idol is anything that takes more priority in your life than God does. Idols work at stripping you of your innocence. Do you know how wonderful it is to get up, preach and not feel any shame? I don't feel guilt. I don't feel condemnation. I don't feel the weight of sin. Some preachers never feel that way. They never walk behind the pulpit with total purity flowing. It was not an easy place to attain. You must do whatever it takes to get back to the place of innocence.

In a previous chapter, I mentioned a company that produced "innocent" children videos. I believe this company is one of the sacred calves that is destroying innocent children today. I believe that prophetically speaking God is asking people all over the world the same questions.

"How long will it take for My children to regain true innocence? Can you see the demonic strongholds that keep you bound? How long before you refuse to bow to them? How long do I have to wait for you to become innocent towards me? How long will you meditate on trash and other image stealers that destroy innocence? How long are you going to defile yourselves with dysfunctional rebellious people and make rebellious covenants with the world? How long is it going to take to attain innocence? If you want My anointing to flow, you must first find the place of innocence", saith the Lord.

God wants to release His miraculous power through us. He wants to move in mighty strength, but He is looking for people who will rise up and walk in innocence towards Him. How long is it going to take the body of Christ to get what they ask for in prayer?

If ye abide in me, and my words abide in you, ye shall ask what ye will, and it shall be done unto you.

John 15:7 (KJV)

That is called innocence. Innocence believes that whatever it asks for it will receive. Innocence doesn't expect the answer "No." Innocence believes that money grows on trees. Imagine growing up with a father who never lacked anything. You would be innocent of poverty and lack. You would believe in blessings and abundance all of the time. Innocence builds strength and fortitude to stand and receive all God has.

I remember praying for a three-year-old boy who had a brain tumor. I commanded the tumor to go. I felt the power of God hit that little boy, but he just stood there. Three months later, he was totally healed. I marveled that he didn't even fall down under the power. He showed none of the outward signs of receiving we've come to expect. God told me that innocence has the ability to receive and contain His power. Did you understand that? I said innocence has the ability to contain power! Innocence creates space for power. In many of our hearts, we have built up resentment and unforgiveness that block the power of God. It stops the power from flowing in and through us. We can't stay like we are and be like our Daddy. Only the pure in heart shall see God (Matthew 5:8). God is looking for a pure heart, because that is where His power can be contained. A pure heart has the ability to receive and contain the power of God.

Chapter 9

Daniel: An Example of Innocence

D aniel is a good example of a man who knew the power of innocence. Daniel was brought into the kingdom of Babylon as a young teenager. Even at that time, something had already been instilled in him that enabled him to have an incredible trust and simplicity of loving reliance upon God. He never compromised. He held to what he had been taught. He fasted. He loved the Lord. He prayed three times a day.

Something powerful was put inside this child that held to such integrity that every time a different king would reign, there was Daniel rising to power beside the king. On his knees three times a day, he would rise before the sun and pray. At noon and at evening he would pray. He flourished in this purity he was taught as a child. His wisdom was incredible. He had vision and understood dreams. He was taken into a Babylonian system but whatever he learned as a child was locked into his spirit.

Then the king commanded, and they brought Daniel, and cast him into the den of lions. Now the king spake and said unto Daniel, Thy God whom thou servest continually, he will deliver thee.

And a stone was brought, and laid upon the mouth of the den; and the king sealed it with his own signet, and with the signet of his lords; that the purpose might not be changed concerning Daniel.

Then the king went to his palace, and passed the night fasting: neither were instruments of musick brought before him: and his sleep went from him.

Then the king arose very early in the morning, and went in haste unto the den of lions.

And when he came to the den, he cried with a lamentable voice unto Daniel: and the king spake and said to Daniel, O Daniel, servant of the living God, is thy God, whom thou servest continually, able to deliver thee from the lions?

Then said Daniel unto the king, O king, live for ever.

My God hath sent his angel, and hath shut the lions' mouths, that they have not hurt me: forasmuch as before him *innocence was found in me;* and also before thee, O king, have I done no hurt.

Then was the king exceeding glad for him, and commanded that they should take Daniel up out of the den. So Daniel was taken up out of the den, and no manner of hurt was found upon him, because he believed in his God.

Daniel 6:16-23

The Book of Daniel tells us why God shut the mouths of the lions — because *innocence was found in him* (verse 23). The lions didn't hurt him because of innocence! That is simplicity of heart and absolute trust in God. I know that wherever I go, my Daddy will protect me. My little boy picked up a spider one day and my wife freaked out. I told her it's all right and told him just to put the thing down. One day in the park he picked up a snake and was playing with it. This is not something that I encouraged him to do, but I did not show fear when he innocently picked up the snake. Everyone else was freaking out that he was playing with a snake. But he just said, "That's okay. If it bites me, I will just shake it off." I didn't teach him to fear. He knows that he has the immunity of the Holy Spirit. He knows if the snake bites him he won't get sick. Innocence is powerful.

Daniel had great confidence and faithfulness instilled into him as a child before he was taken into Babylon. Someone influential in his childhood, maybe his parents or a Rabbi, taught him to understand the power of a relationship with God. He obviously learned divine submission to authority because he always knew how to abide within the structures of every kingdom he worked in. He always rose to the top. He walked in faithfulness, integrity and wisdom (Daniel 6:3). Nothing evil could be found in him (Daniel 6:4). He kept his heart pure. I believe the understanding Daniel had of God gave him the power to maintain such innocence in every experience throughout his life — even through the midst of a lion's den.

Innocence has a unique way of shutting down the voice of the devil. When someone stays innocent, he is protected from a critical spirit. Innocent people are protected from hurt. Theirs is a freedom of joy without asking. Innocence makes one free of fear. Innocence does not carry guilt, shame or condemnation. Daniel said God shut the mouths of the lions because innocence was found in him. Where are the lions in your life? The devil goes about as a roaring lion seeking whom he may devour. But if you remain innocent, there won't be anything to devour.

God pleaded Daniel's cause because of innocence. Nowhere in Scripture do we find that Daniel said anything in his own defense. He left it up to God to clear his name when his integrity was questioned. God didn't take Daniel out of his circumstances, but He miraculously preserved Daniel's life. None of Daniel's actions had offended either God or the king. Daniel did not pretend to be something he was not, but allowed the testimony of his pure conscience to make it clear that he meant offense to no one.

When Daniel came out of the lion's den, he said to his king "O king live forever, the Lord shut the mouths of the lions because innocence was found in me." The word "innocence" found here is the Aramic word "zakuw" which means *purity and innocence*. He was pure. He was holy. He had integrity of character. He had absolute trust and reliance upon God. The power of innocence will shut the mouths of lions.

God preserved his life by a miracle. Darius said, "... thy God whom you serve continually..." (verse 20), to which Daniel replies to the king, "My God sent his angel, and he shut the mouths of the lions...because I was found innocent in his sight" (verse 22 *NIV*).

The same bright and glorious being seen with the three Hebrew children in the fiery furnace (Daniel 3:20) had visited Daniel and kept him company all night. He shut the mouths of the lions so they had could not hurt Daniel in any manner.

God's power restrains the roaring lion that goes about continually seeking to devour the Father's children. Can you see the care God takes of His faithful worshippers? He will keep our souls from sin, comfort us with His peace and receive us to Himself. In our innocence, we can *expect* Him to shut the mouths of lions.

How can you successfully handle God's unlimited power, anointing, wisdom and resources? Only an innocence heart can create room for unlimited power. Innocence has the capacity to contain and withstand unlimited power.

Conclusion
The Power of Innocence

I heard a story of a vision the Lord gave to a man one time. It was about a powerful huge red bull that ate all the right nutrients to make him strong and capable. The Lord showed the man that he was the bull. He had all this power and strength and really thought he was something. Then, he was given a gift he could not unwrap. He tossed it around with his horn and tried with all his might to unwrap it. But he couldn't do it. Then he watched a nine-month old child come along, began to tear at the paper and easily unwrapped the gift. Out of that box came all the gifts of the spirit...casting out devils...healing the sick. The power to raise the dead was in that box. All the powers of heaven were there as he sat in absolute amazement. The Lord showed him the simplicity of innocence is all that is needed to unwrap the great powers of heaven.

Innocence can grab hold, unlock, and open the powers of heaven to do every mighty sign and wonder. The powers of heaven will not be unwrapped by knowledge and education. It is a simple innocence that says, "I love you, Lord." The pure in heart shall see God. When you see His face, you see power. It will establish a great innocence within you. You simply believe because He is your daddy. And mighty miracles begin to happen. It isn't complicated. We make the powers of heaven more complicated than they are. We have allowed the enemy to cloud our minds and strip us of the ability to see ourselves as children and sons of God. As long as Christians are deceived, they can never walk in what God has designed for them. The devil is trying to steal your purity. Can you see it?

God showed this man the answer to loosing God's creative miracles through this vision. They are only unlocked by innocence. That is why God says to wash your hands with innocence. That is why He wants you to return and find the place of innocence. When you wash your hands in innocence, you will see His power flow.

God is trying to restore innocence to the body of Christ. He told us in His Word that we would only possess the Kingdom of Heaven as a child. The Kingdom of God is within us. We must believe it is that natural and simple. Believe your Daddy. Believe you can cast out devils, heal the sick and raise the dead. Believe it!

If we are not willing to be holy as He is holy (1 Peter 1:6), then we can't expect God to move in massive power. We need to find a place where our conscience is absolutely cleared and we know it is totally innocent before God.

Put these words in your spirit and pray this prayer with me.

"Father, create in me a clean heart, O God, and renew in me a steadfast spirit. I pray you begin to restore innocence in the body of Christ right now. Help me grasp the simplicity of being your child and believing that everything of Yours is mine. I don't have to get stressed and anxious about anything because I know that You, Father, are my Daddy. You, alone, know exactly what I need and what is good for me. You know how to train and discipline me. I pray that every word will

sink deep into my spirit and revelation will come out of the purity and simplicity of Your heart into mine. In Jesus name, let me be Your child. Train me to be the child You have called me to be. Begin the restoration of innocence within me now. Thank you, Jesus."

Now just lift your hands and begin to worship the Father. Allow Him to minister to you right now.

If you need prayer, or agreement in prayer, please call or write our office.

Sword Ministries International
PMB 649
3044 Shepherd of the Hills Exp. Suite 100
Branson, MO 65616
417-335-7650
Or you can contact us through our web site at:
www.swordministries.org

We Would Like
To Hear
From You!

My staff and I at Sword Ministries believe that through reading this book you were touched by the power and glory of God. It is important to us and to the Lord that you let us know what wonderful things God is doing for you, and how your life was changed. Please send us your testimony so others can see what God has done for you. We would love to hear from you soon and we look forward to reading your testimony.

In addition, we would also like you to pray about becoming a *VISIONARY COVENANT PARTNER* with all of us at Sword Ministries International. As you join with us, it will enable us to touch more lives with the power and glory of God. In Philippians chapter 4, Paul speaks about becoming a partaker of grace. As you become a part of this ministry in prayer and finances you will become a partaker of the grace that God has given to us.

As you pray, we believe that you will be sensitive to the leading of the Holy Spirit on whether you are to become a part of this ministry. We believe that you have been blessed mightily by this book and believe that your life has been changed. To become a vital part of this ministry please fill out this form and send it with your prayer request and financial support to the address on the following page.

Clip & Mail
to the
Address Below

☐ I would like to become a partner with your ministry.
Enclosed is my offering of $_____

Thank you for your support of this ministry. I know that
you will be abundantly blessed through your giving.

Name_____

Address_____

City_____

State_____ Zip _____

Credit Card# _____

Exp Date_____Visa_____MC_____

Clip & Mail To:

SWORD MINISTRIES
PMB 649
3044 Shepherd of the Hills Exprwy # 100
Branson, MO 65616
Phone: 417-335-7650 • Fax: 417-334-2003
E-mail Address: SWORD352@AOL.COM
World Wide Web: www.swordministries.org

Keys That Will Unlock the Kingdom

Keys to a Yielded Will

In a fresh new light, Warren Hunter explores biblical truth's that will help individuals become vessels that are completely yielded and ready for the greatest outpouring of His spirit the world has ever seen.

$7.00

Presenting a Yielded Will

In the sequel to "Keys to a Yielded Will", Warren reveals how our salvation really hung in the balance of Jesus' life. One single act of disobedience would have nullified the power of His sacrifice. How many people are hanging in the balance at this time? Waiting on the obedience of our yielded will?

$8.00

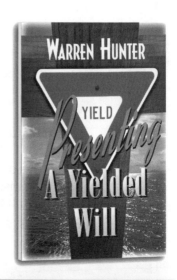

ORDER FORM

Name_____

Address_____

City_____

State_____ Zip _____

Credit Card# _____

Exp Date_____Visa_____MC_____

Visionary Covenant Partner

☐ I would like to become a Visionary Covenant Partner.
Enclosed is my first gift of...

☐ 25   ☐ 50   ☐ 100   ☐ 250
☐ 500   ☐ 750   ☐ 1000   ☐ 5000

Or Other $_____ (Please fill in amout in Partner Gift Below)

		Shipping & Handling USA Only
Product Cost	$ _____	Under $10............Add $2.00
S&H	$ _____	$10-$20.................Add $4.00
Sub Total	$ _____	$21-$30.................Add $6.00
Partner Gift	$ _____	$31-$40.................Add $7.00
		$41-$50.................Add $8.00
Total Enclosed	$ _____	$51 and Up..........Add 15%

Return Policy: Return any Defective Merchandise within 15 days of receipt.
PLEASE ALLOW 4 - 6 WEEKS FOR DELIVERY
ALL ORDERS MUST BE PREPAID

Clip & Mail To:

SWORD MINISTRIES
PMB 649
3044 Shepherd of the Hills Exprwy # 100
Branson, MO 65616
Phone: 417-335-7650 • Fax: 417-334-2003
E-mail Address: SWORD352@AOL.COM
World Wide Web: www.swordministries.org

Single Tapes

	Full of New Wine	$5.00
	The Ultimate Weapon	$5.00
	Journey of the Glory	$5.00
	The Breath of God	$5.00
	Divine Compassion	$5.00
	5 A's & 3 R's	$5.00
	In Christ Dwells Fulness	$5.00
	Take Time to Get Fire	$5.00
	The Promised Seal	$5.00
	New Testament Church	$5.00
	Unlimited Seed of Christ	$5.00
	Controlling Your Dreams	$5.00
	Proclaiming Christ	$5.00
	Voice of the Lord	$5.00
	Fueling for Fire	$5.00
	Praying for Revival	$5.00
	Flames of Intercession	$5.00
	Ephesians 1:18	$5.00
	Face to Face	$5.00
	Heart to Heart	$5.00
	The Hand of God	$5.00
	Preach Christ	$5.00
	Anointed Blood	$5.00
	Anointed Body	$5.00
	Sanctified Tongue	$5.00
	Sanctified Body	$5.00
	Glory of Hope	$5.00
	Called Out of The Familiar	$5.00

Single Tapes cont.

	Seeing Impartation	$5.00
	Seeing Past Death	$5.00
	Foundation for Prayer	$5.00
	Spread Your Wings	$5.00
	Cornelius Doorway to Power	$5.00
	Walk on the Water	$5.00
	Wrapped in His Presence	$5.00
	The Eagle Speaks	$5.00
	Redemptive Revelation -K. Hunter	$5.00
	What are You Yoked With -K.Hunter	$5.00
	Valleys -K.Hunter	$5.00
	Identifying the Gehazi -K.Hunter	$5.00
	Faith Without Works is Dead -K.Hunter	$5.00
	The Battle of the Gods	$5.00
	The Ultimate Decision	$5.00
	First Fruits	$5.00
	A Giving Eye	$5.00
	Seed of Covenant	$5.00
	Personhood of the Glory	$5.00

Books

	Keys To A Yielded Will	$7.00
	Presenting A Yielded Will	$8.00
	Unlimited Realm Vol. 1	$7.00
	From Fire To Glory	$10.00
	Transparency	$7.00
	Is Your Perception A Weapon?	$8.00
	Growing In Confidence	$7.00
	Power Of A Consecrated Heart	$7.00

Books cont.

	Supply Of The Spirit	$8.00
	Touch Not Mine Anointed	$6.00
	Vision Of The Seed	$6.00
	Glory Of The Anointing	$7.00
	Weightiness of God	$6.00
	Visionaries Rise To Leadership	$7.00
	Visionaries Set Your Sights Higher	$7.00
	Unlimited Realm Vol. 2	$7.00
	Buy All 16 Books and Save 30% Off!	$80.00

Album Tape Sets   Buy Any 3 and Get 20% Off!

	16 Classic Tapes	16 Tapes	$70.00
	Moving in Supernatural	16 Tapes	$70.00
	Power of Covenant	15 Tapes	$65.00
	Secrets of Financial Freedom	12 Tapes	$60.00
	God Working With God	12 Tapes	$60.00
	Be Son of God You Are	10 Tapes	$50.00
	Called to Call	10 Tapes	$50.00
	Meditating God's Thoughts	9 Tapes	$45.00
	Love's Perception	9 Tapes	$45.00
	Mirror of Grace	8 Tapes	$40.00
	Following the Cloud	8 Tapes	$40.00
	Anointed Ones Anointing	8 Tapes	$40.00
	Love's Destiny	8 Tapes	$40.00
	Financial Dominion	8 Tapes	$40.00
	Transparency	7 Tapes	$35.00
	Visionary Leadership	7 Tapes	$35.00
	Manifesting Life	7 Tapes	$35.00
	Yield To Healing	7 Tapes	$35.00
	Supply of The Spirit	7 Tapes	$35.00

Album Tape Sets   Buy Any 3 and Get 20% Off!

	Growing In Revival	6 Tapes	$30.00
	Recovery of Sight to the Blind	6 Tapes	$30.00
	Fruity Weapons **NEW!**	6 Tapes	$30.00
	Come Forth to Power	6 Tapes	$30.00
	Healing Absolutes	6 Tapes	$30.00
	New Realms of Vision	6 Tapes	$30.00
	Don't Abort A Miracle	6 Tapes	$30.00
	Fire to Glory	6 Tapes	$30.00
	Emanating the Anointing	6 Tapes	$30.00
	Apostolic Power Base	6 Tapes	$30.00
	Apostolic Patterns Vol. 1 **NEW!**	6 Tapes	$30.00
	Apostolic Patterns Vol. 2 **NEW!**	5 Tapes	$25.00
	Champions	5 Tapes	$25.00
	Angels	5 Tapes	$25.00
	Uncapping the Forces of God	5 Tapes	$25.00
	Power of Confidence	5 Tapes	$25.00
	Mystery of Godliness	5 Tapes	$25.00
	Retrofit	5 Tapes	$25.00
	Consecrated Heart	5 Tapes	$25.00
	Abolishing Death **NEW!**	4 Tapes	$20.00
	Miracle Seed Harvest	4 Tapes	$20.00
	Intimacy With God	4 Tapes	$20.00
	Perceptions Image	4 Tapes	$20.00
	The Intercession of Jesus	4 Tapes	$20.00
	Meditating on Supernatural	4 Tapes	$20.00
	Power of Obedience **NEW!**	4 Tapes	$20.00
	Ephesians Chapter One	4 Tapes	$20.00
	Fire is Your Future	4 Tapes	$20.00

Album Tape Sets   Buy Any 3 and Get 20% Off!

	Christ the Hope of Glory	4 Tapes	$20.00
	Unlimited Realm Vol. 1	4 Tapes	$20.00
	Weightiness of God	4 Tapes	$20.00
	Divine Capabilities	4 Tapes	$20.00
	Leading With Power	3 Tapes	$15.00
	The Order of Faith	3 Tapes	$15.00
	Glory of The Anointing	3 Tapes	$15.00
	Unlimited Realm Vol. 2	3 Tapes	$15.00
	Crucifixion of Empathy	3 Tapes	$15.00
	Purity -K. Hunter	3 Tapes	$15.00
	Breaking Selfishness	3 Tapes	$15.00
	Getting Dressed Power	3 Tapes	$15.00
	Prophetic Indicators	3 Tapes	$15.00
	Unlimited Finances	2 Tapes	$10.00
	Ephesians 3:17	2 Tapes	$10.00
	Vessels of Destiny	2 Tapes	$10.00
	Presenting A Yielded Will	2 Tapes	$10.00
	Power of Innocence	2 Tapes	$10.00
	Love Greatest Weapon	2 Tapes	$10.00
	Why People Get Sick?	2 Tapes	$10.00
	Ishmael & Isaac Miracle	2 Tapes	$10.00
	Men Maneuvered Devil	2 Tapes	$10.00
	Hiding in Christ -K. Hunter	2 Tapes	$10.00
	Confession Declares Position	2 Tapes	$10.00
	The Greatest Thing I Value **NEW!**	2 Tapes	$10.00

The Vision of Sword Ministries

The foundation of this ministry rests in Hebrews 4:12 which is summarized in the following statement, "Speaking the Truth in Revival, Piercing the Innermost Being." We are to remain carriers of revival, "Demonstrating Signs and Wonders, Decently and In Order, by the Power of the Holy Spirit."

Our vision is to see the stadiums of America and around the world filled to capacity in which the fullness of the Gospel of Christ, the Anointed One is declared unto salvation. Not just in persuasive words of man's wisdom, but in demonstration of the Spirit and in Power (Acts 2), which includes salvation according to Acts 10:44.

To see multitudes touched by the loving presentation of the power of God through power packed spirit filled books published in many different languages, world wide multi-media television and radio productions, and churches and Bible schools established in China and other nations, via Apostolic teams and multi-faceted Evangelistic operations.